Love, Lo
Everything Inbetween

Bethany O'Connor

BookLeaf
Publishing

Love, Loss and Everything Inbetween ©
2022 Bethany O'Connor

All rights reserved.

Bethany O'Connor asserts the moral right to
be identified as author of this work.

Presentation by *BookLeaf Publishing*

Web: www.bookleafpub.com

E-mail: info@bookleafpub.com

ISBN: 978-93-95950-67-1

First edition 2022

To those all those that have been loved and lost along the way... Always in our hearts.

She was poetry

She was poetry...
The way the universe knew she was too good;
The way the stars were jealous of her shine,
And the way the sun was outshone by her
radiance.

She was poetry...
Even when she left.
These walls still whisper her name,
The bed sheets cling onto her scent.

She was poetry...
My heart left with hers;
But still I sigh her name.
My words will never be enough but may they
serve as a reminder;

She was poetry, and I am just the writer

Disquiet demons

I know getting through this can be daunting;
You face the fears in your mind,
The demons in your soul,
And the disquiet in your heart.
But know that I will fight these disquiet
fearsome demons with you.
I will love you on the days when you don't want
to be loved.
I will hold you during the times you think you
are not enough.
I will carry your pieces, love your parts, cherish
your scars.
In the end you will see that you are enough, that
those demons twisted your thoughts into lies.
And I will be here,
Helping you banish the darkness from your
burdened soul.

Hello darkness, my old friend

The darkness comes to me like a familiar face;
A heavy blanket.
Are you keeping me warm or trying to smother
me?

I feel pushed deeper into the void;
The aching pit of despair.
I know it well here.
I see past versions of myself in the wreckage.
They scream at me for not learning how to avoid
this dungeon.

I am welcomed by all the thoughts that I have
tried to avoid.
The thoughts that never really left;
They merely hid in the corners of my mind,
Awaiting vulnerability
They demand to be heard.

The darkness surrounds me.
It's like a thick tar;
Dragging me deeper into it with sticky clutches,
Blocking my airways, infesting my insides.

I'm too tired of fighting this saga.
My body aches, my mind exhausted, my will
driven out by persistent dark chaos.
You win this time darkness;
You have sunk my sanity.

Preacher

If there comes a day when you think that you are
not worthy,
Come to me and I will preach to you your
wonders.

Soul Searcher

Maybe we're all just broken souls,
Trying to find something that makes us feel alive
again.

Heart and Soul

Heart of a romantic;
Soul of a poet.

I was always doomed to feel too much.

Surplus love

And when you are unable to love yourself;
I will love you enough for the two of us.

Don't look back now darling

Looking through old posts and being reminded
of the despair I was feeling a few years ago...
Posts about suicide,
Posts about self-harm,
Posts about never feeling worthy,
Posts about not wanting to be alive.

It hurts to be reminded of the pain I was feeling.
In the depths of my depression and self-loathing.
Thoughts of escaping the abyss were my only
companion.

The ache of remembering my negative thoughts
and swirling darkness inside my mind.
If I could go back, I would tell you to hold on.
Don't think about those things that will do you
harm.
It will not take the pain away.

I would tell you that you make it;
Scathed and scarred, but very much alive.
I would tell you that you find love;
A love that will aid the healing.

But most of all I would tell you;
You are worthy. You are loved. You are fearless.
And one day you will know that this is enough.

Wish you were here

I'm not quite sure how I'm here without you.
How am I here living, breathing, existing,
without you.
Everyday since you left has felt different,
Empty. Hollow. Lifeless.

I forgive you for leaving us, for leaving me...
But sometimes I still get angry.
The thoughts pounding my mind, asking the
same questions again and again;
Why did you do it? How could you do it? Did
you not know how much we loved you? How
much we still love you...

You gave the world the version of you that you
could.
A laugh that lit up the room and eyes blue
enough to fall into.
You were too pure and you felt too much.
I saw the crushing weight of it on you,
Saw the toll it took,
Relentless misery and turmoil.

So yes,
I do forgive you. Some days more than others.

But by God, does my chest ache for you.
Part of me left that day with you.
Treasure it and keep it safe,
For I will always keep you with me.

Fire starter

The way you love me starts a fire in my veins;
Set me ablaze with a kiss and I will burn forever
with you.

My love

I have never felt more loved than when I'm with you.
You can make my heart stop with a single glance;
You fill me joy every time you smile.

The memories of us laughing will be burned in my mind forever.
The way your eyes light up.
Laughing until we can't breath.
I want to hear that laugh for the rest of my life.

Borderline Personality
Disaster

The nails they dig beneath your skin,
Roaches, maggots, come on in.
My graveyard lullaby grants eternal sleep,
To any useless, worthless, braindead sheep.

Gaze at the coffin, get inside,
Make peace with God and say goodnight.
The horror of my thoughts give me such a fright,
So we must medicate and keep it locked inside.

Borderline personality disaster,
Borderline personality disaster.
Is this the kind of sin you were after...

I'm not schizophrenic, I just have the vision

Wake from your dreaded sleep,
You feel oh so weak.
There's so much poison around,
I'll have my fill then meet the ground.

We've lost something that we love,
Until that we will become.
Ye of little faith is bound,
To a casket put straight in the ground.

With a thousand eyes to see,
With the end I see so near.
With a thousand ears to hear,
Chances to manipulate me.
Can we just run and not look back
Until our world just fades to black.
I'll hold your hand, you're safe with me.

It's been a fight just to be here,
Overcome from what I have done,
For what I will do...

There's so much poison around,
I'll have my fill then meet the ground.

And it's me choosing you,
You best not refuse.

Ye of little faith is bound,
To a casket put straight in the ground.

Unstable Supernova- My brightest star

I think that I was better off without you,
Turns out all I ever did was doubt you,
Like you did me.

You know I'm oh so traumatised
And blinded by your pretty lies.
You go and live your eccentric life,
While I stay institutionalised.

Wait for me, I can't catch up.
I'm a fuck up and you know that.
Wait and see, I'll be the brightest star,
Unstable supernova.

Some days I can't escape my head,
All days I just long for death.
Some days I take too many meds,
Then I'm back in the ambulance.

Gravity

Space has always been a curiosity to me.
To wonder what it would be like to see stars
implode;
Black holes inhaling everything around them.
To feel the full force of gravity dragging all that
remains into the void.

But this darkness is still a thing of marvel and
beauty;
Terror and magnificence.
Then I look at you,
Green eyes, oh so divine.
And I feel a fraction of this marvel.

I look at you and my heart implodes,
I am now the stars being dragged into void,
The strength of your gaze drawing me into the
abyss of your love.

There is no force strong enough to hold me back
from you.
You are my gravity.

Home

I didn't know that a person could feel like home,
but you;
I find comfort in your arms,
Peace in your company,
Happiness in your smile.
You light up everyday with a word, a look, a
fleeting touch of your hand.
Your love ripples in the creases of my smile.
Your heartbeat etched on my soul.

Kaleidoscope eyes

Some people have kaleidoscopes in their eyes...
They see what we see,
But never in the same way.

They see magic in the ordinary.
Beauty in the bleak.

These are the people to surround yourself with.
The people that can see you for your
magnificence.

"I feel infinite"

Windows down,
Summer sun beaming down.
Driving home to the woman I love,
Music blaring.

I think to one of my favourite quotes:
"I feel infinite".
The phrase has stuck with me for years;
Through the days when the darkness consumed
me,
And the days where my soul wasn't as heavy.

Driving home: I feel infinite.
A day where I feel that I can take on the world.
I look at my life, I see my blessings.

Things are good.

Milton Keynes UK
Ingram Content Group UK Ltd.
UKHW020756080124
435661UK00018B/1180